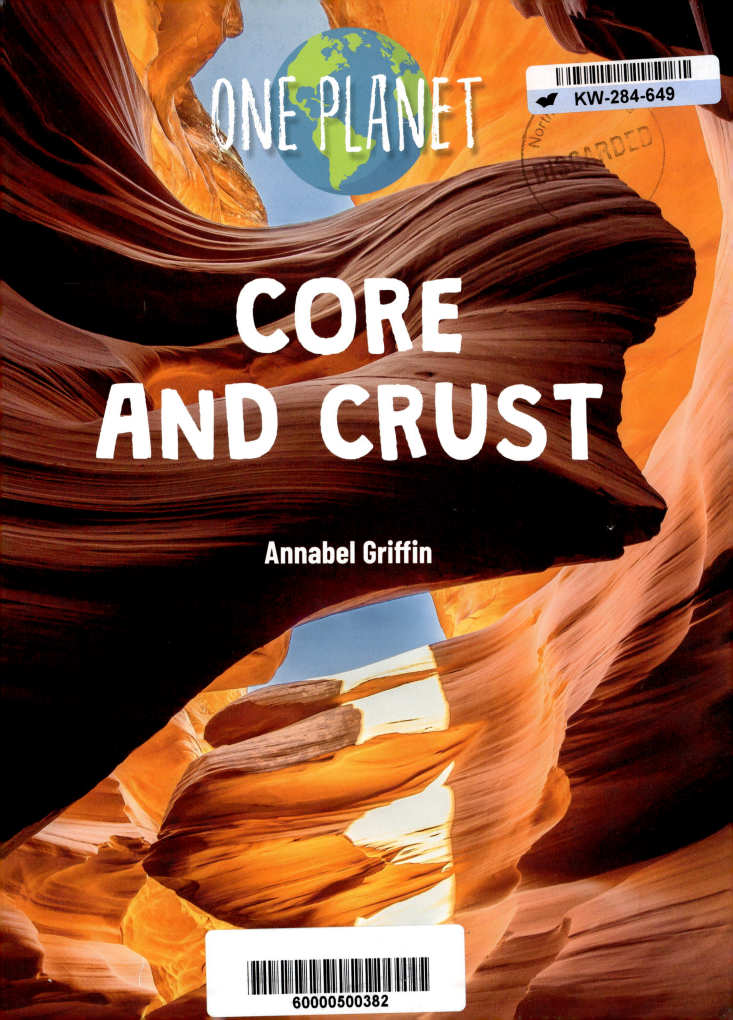

ONE PLANET

CORE AND CRUST

Annabel Griffin

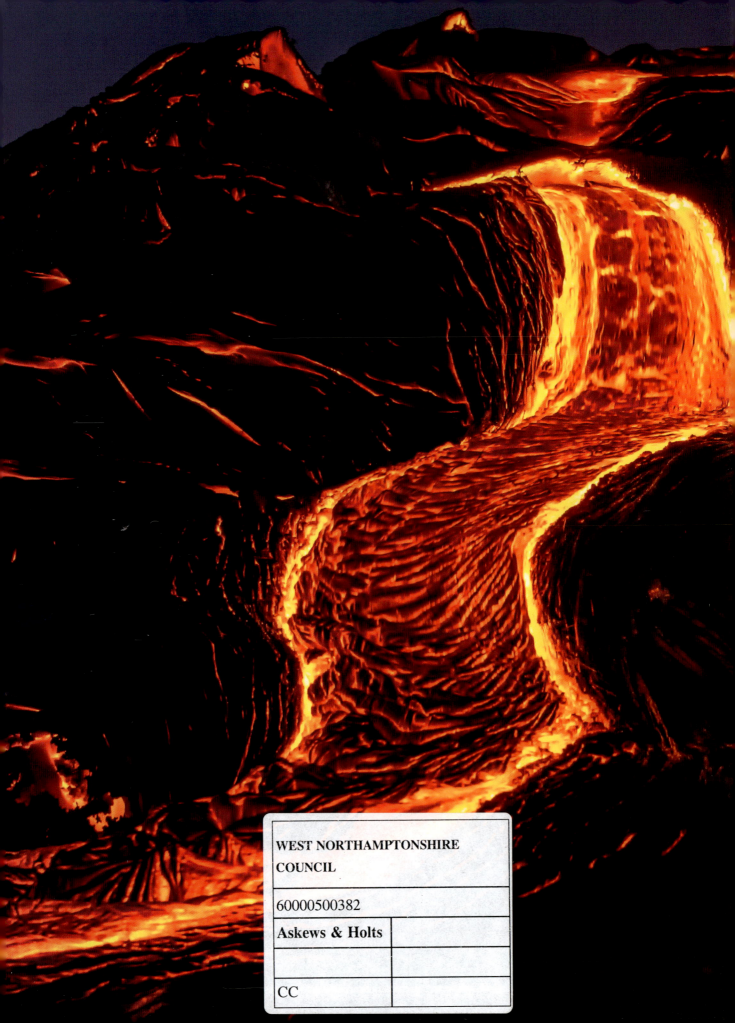

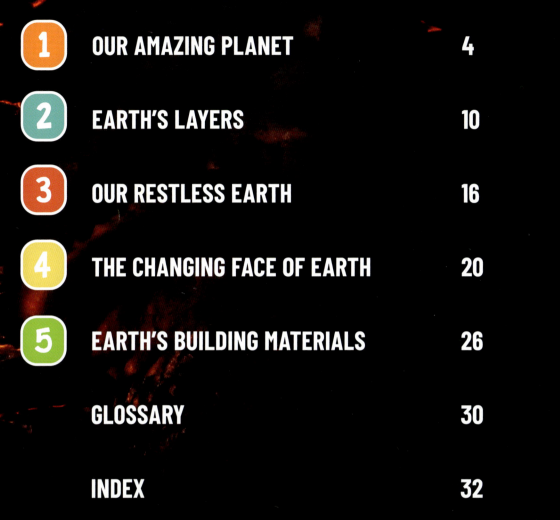

CONTENTS

First published by Hungry Tomato Ltd in 2022
F1, Old Bakery Studios, Blewetts Wharf, Malpas Road, Truro, Cornwall, TR1 1QH, UK.

Copyright © Hungry Tomato Ltd 2022

www.hungrytomato.com

ISBN 978 1 914087 936

A CIP catalogue record for this book is available from the British Library

Printed in China

Picture credits (t=top; b=bottom; c=centre; l=left; r=right; bg=background)

Corbis 23bl. istock 15cr. NASA 7br, 29tl. National Oceanic and Atmospheric Administration 21br. NHPA 19l. PlanetObserver – www. planetobserver.com 17b. Science Photo Library 15bl, 22b, 28bg, 28tl, 28cl. Shutterstock: 13b; 17tr; 26bl; 24K-Production 4bg; Alex GK Lee 8bg; alysta 24br; Amanda Mohler 10-11b; Amy Nichole Harris 9tr; beboy 20bg; CAN BALCIOGLU 5cr; canadastock 1bg; charles taylor 9cr; CHULKOVA NINA 20bl; Cristiano Pereira Ribeiro 26tl; Designua 16b; Eugene Buchko 27bl; Galyna Andrushko 24bg; GybasDigiPhoto 9br; I. Pilon 14tr; IrinaK 6bg; Jakub Cejpek 8bl; Jamey Ekins 16tl; Jaroslaw Grudzinski 5tr; jmb 21tr; Larsek 7tr; Mirenska Olga 11cr; Momentum 10tl; Romolo Tavani 4l; SciePro 5br, 7cr; sootra 10cl; Spectral-Design 29tr; Stacey Bates 14b; T.mar 6tl; travis manley 19tr; VectorMine 13tc; Yvonne Baur 2bg. Superstock: 6bl, 12bg, 21cr, 25tr.

Every effort has been made to trace the copyright holders, and we apologise in advance for any unintentional omissions. We would be pleased to insert the appropriate acknowledgments in any subsequent edition of this publication.

1. OUR AMAZING PLANET

Our Earth is a ball of rock hurtling through space at around 67,000 miles per hour (108,000 km/h). Using satellites, we can see the surface of our Earth from space. Its rocky surface is covered in vast blue stretches of water, surrounding great landmasses. If we move closer, we can see towering rocky mountains and deep valleys, and large areas of green vegetation.

Birth of the Planet

Our planet's history began over 4.5 billion years ago. Scientists believe that at that time our solar system was just a huge cloud of dust and gas floating in space. Then the cloud began to collapse and the dust and gas spiralled inward.

Out of this came a newly formed star – our Sun. Some of the dust particles that were left spinning around the Sun began to stick together. They formed large chunks of rock. Some of these rocks were small enough to fit in your hand. Others were as large as mountains. These rocky chunks joined together and grew until they became rocky planets. One of these planets became Earth.

The Moon is located 238,855 miles (384,400 km) from the Earth.

Birth of the Moon

The Moon is Earth's only natural satellite. Scientists believe the Moon formed not too long after the Earth, when one of the huge whirling masses of rock circling the Sun collided with Earth. Debris from the collision exploded into space and began circling Earth, and then joined together to form the Moon.

Planet Earth is about 93 million miles (150 million kilometres) from the Sun. It is the third planet from the Sun in our solar system. This perfect position keeps the temperature of our planet moderate and stable. This is one of the reasons why life is possible on Earth.

White clouds float in the atmosphere (the layer of gases that surrounds our planet).

PLANET EARTH FACTS

Earth's Ingredients

Most of the Earth is made up of just eight elements: aluminum, calcium, iron, magnesium, oxygen, potassium, silicon, and sodium. Silicon and oxygen make up about 75% of Earth's rock.

The Blue Planet

Earth is a unique planet in our solar system. It is the only planet to have large quantities of liquid water on its surface. Without this water there would be no life on Earth.

An Earth Year

It takes the Earth 365 days, 6 hours, 9 minutes and 10 seconds to orbit the Sun. To complete one orbit, the Earth travels about 584 million miles (940 million kilometres).

Earth's Early Years

As debris from space continued to pound the young planet Earth, its surface heated and melted. Eventually, scientists believe, it was a huge sea of molten rock and metal. Each new bit of matter added to the mix and increased the planet's size.

At the same time, the molten rock released nitrogen, carbon dioxide and water vapor into the air. The stream of debris also added lots of dust to the mix. An atmosphere was forming around the planet, but it was a dark, dusty, and poisonous one!

Scientists are not sure when Earth's surface began to form a crust and start to solidify, but rocks about 3.8 billion years old have been found in Canada.

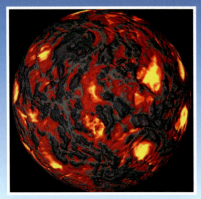

This artwork shows the Earth as it may have looked during its molten phase.

Extinction Level Event

The Chicxulub Crater in Mexico has an impact crater of around 106 miles (170 km) in diameter. Scientists believe the impact was caused by an asteroid or meteorite with a diameter of about 6.2 miles (10 km)! The impact happened about 65 million years ago and would have caused earthquakes, firestorms, tsunamis and catastrophic devastation on the Earth's surface. Some scientists believe this collision with space debris caused the extinction of the dinosaurs.

Meteorites

Today, bits of rock and metal are still shooting through space. Most of these pieces of space debris burn up when they hit the Earth's atmosphere. But sometimes they make it to the surface. When they do, we call them meteorites.

Earth's crust is marked by craters from prehistoric meteorite collisions. Scientists estimate that over the past billion years there have been about 130,000 impacts that have produced craters with a diameter of 0.6 miles (1 km) or larger.

The Meteor Crater in Arizona, USA, was formed between 20,000 and 50,000 years ago. The crater measures 0.7 miles (1.2 km) in diameter. It was made by an asteroid measuring about 24 metres (79 feet) in diameter. It was the first crater on Earth to be identified as an impact crater.

SPACE DEBRIS

Meteors/Meteorites

Meteors are chunks of rock and metal. As they enter Earth's atmosphere, they burn up and make a streak of light. When they do this we call them shooting stars. A meteor that hits Earth is known as a meteorite.

Asteroids

Asteroids are jagged, rocky bodies. Most are found orbiting the Sun in an area called the 'asteroid belt', between Mars and Jupiter. Some asteroids can be nearly 621 miles (1,000 km) wide.

Comets

Comets are balls of frozen gas, dust and rock that orbit the Sun. As a comet gets close to the Sun, some of the ice on its surface evaporates. This releases dust to form a tail. A comet's dust tail can be 6 million miles (10 million kilometres) long.

PLANET EARTH: INSIDE AND OUT

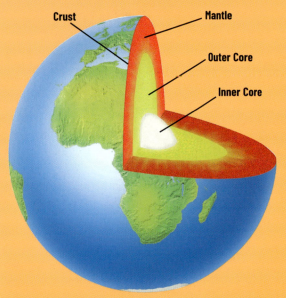

Crust

Mantle

Outer Core

Inner Core

Diameter at the Equator:
7,926 miles (12,756 km)

Diameter at the Poles:
7,900 miles (12,714 km)

Circumference at the Equator:
23,627 miles (38,024 km)

Weight (Mass) of the Earth:
7.3 sextillion tons
(6.5 sextillion metric tonnes)

Distance from the Sun:
93 million miles (150 million km)

Average surface temperature:
15°C (79°F)

The Planet as We Know It

Earth's surfaces began to cool and form a crust. But even then, the planet remained molten inside. Melted rock, called magma, churned and flowed.

All of this heat and movement released huge amounts of water vapor into the young planet's atmosphere and more water was brought to the planet by comets.

The water gathered in the atmosphere only to rain back down onto the planet. Low spots

Not a Perfect Sphere

Mount Chimborazo, in Ecuador, South America, sits on the Equator. The diameter of the Earth is greater at the Equator than at the poles. Therefore, the top of Mount Chimborazo is actually the furthest point from the centre of the Earth!

in the Earth's surface filled with water, and oceans, lakes and rivers developed. Earth, as we know it, began to take shape.

Today, our active planet is still cooling. But between its birth and today, Earth's structure has divided into three distinct layers. We call these the crust, the mantle, and the core. Below the crust, magma still flows, and sometimes even bursts through to the surface.

Kilauea Volcano, on the Hawaiian Islands' 'Big Island' pours molten lava into the ocean. Today, volcanoes are a constant reminder of the continued activity beneath Earth's crust.

OUR MOLTEN EARTH

Shaping from Within

Here magma can be seen beneath the Earth's crust. Lava is magma that has reached Earth's surface. When the lava pours from beneath Earth's crust it shapes the surface. This is one of the ways that scientists believe the planet developed.

Adding to the Landscape

New lava flows out of and over previous flows. Just as with Earth's early crust, the lava cools and hardens at uneven speeds.

New Terrain

These plants are growing on a hillside formed from cooled lava and volcanic ash. After a volcano erupts, water, wind, heat and cold will break down the rocks and carry in sand and debris. Patches of soil will form where seeds can grow.

HIGHS AND LOWS

Mount Everest

Mount Everest is a peak in the Himalayan Mountains, located between Nepal and Tibet in Asia. It is the highest point on Earth, standing at 8,849 metres (29,032 feet) tall.

The Dead Sea

The lowest point on Earth not covered by water or ice is along the shore of the Dead Sea. This salty inland sea borders Israel and Jordan. The shore is around 400 metres (1,300 feet) below sea level.

ASIA   Japan

Challenger Deep
● Trench

Indonesia

AUSTRALIA

Challenger Deep

If we include places on the Earth's crust that are under the ocean, then the Challenger Deep is the lowest point below sea level. This section of the Marianas Ocean Trench is in the northwest Pacific Ocean and is 10,924 metres (35,840 feet) deep.

2. EARTH'S LAYERS

Earth's crust is the most visible part of the planet and the part we know best. The soaring mountains, deep valleys, and seemingly bottomless ocean trenches make the Earth's crust seem 'rock solid' and almost indestructible. In reality, the crust is the thinnest and most fragile of Earth's layers. If you think of the Earth as an apple, then the crust is like the apple's skin!

The Grand Canyon, in Arizona, USA, allows us to see deep into the Earth's layered crust. The canyon is 277 miles (446 km) long and about 1,829 metres (6,001 feet) deep at its lowest point.

Earth's Brittle Crust

The Earth's landscape is quite different from place to place. This means the thickness of the crust is also different. It is thicker where there are high mountains, and thinner in deep trenches. Beneath the oceans the crust is generally about 4.3 miles (7 km) thick. Where there are landmasses, the crust is an average depth of about 24 miles (40 km). Because the planet is covered by so much water, 70 percent of the Earth's crust is under oceans.

EARTH'S CRUST: THICK OR THIN?

The Earth's crust is probably around 25 miles (40 km) thick where you live. To understand the thickness of Earth's crust, try comparing it to something you know.

1) Next time you go on a car journey make a note of the mileage at the start of the trip. Note where you are after driving for 25 miles (40 km). That's how far you would have to travel if you were driving down through the Earth's crust.

2) Locate your hometown on a map. Then find another city, town, or place you know that's about 25 miles (40 km) away.

?

What do you think about Earth's crust now? Thick or thin?

The Mantle

The mantle is the layer beneath the crust. It is the thickest of Earth's layers with an average depth of around 1,800 miles (2,900 km). It is thought to be made mainly of silicon and oxygen.

Upper Mantle

The uppermost layer of the mantle is rigid like the Earth's crust. Below this is the thin asthenosphere layer. At this sub-layer, it starts to get very hot. Temperatures may reach 870°C (1,598°F) – hot enough to melt rocks!

Scientists believe that the asthenosphere is generally semi-solid. But, under heat and pressure, it can become soft enough to flow – slowly. Then it may be more like honey or melted tar.

Hot Spots

A hot spot is an especially hot upper mantle area. Hot spots form when magma from the Earth's mantle rises to the surface. People in Iceland enjoy the benefits of living on a hot spot. Boiling magma close to the surface naturally heats lakes and pools. People can swim outdoors even in winter!

This is the Svartsengi power station in Iceland. Here, steam from the natural hot water is used to power turbines to produce environmentally-friendly electricity. Swimmers enjoy the naturally warm water, too.

THE EARTH'S MANTLE

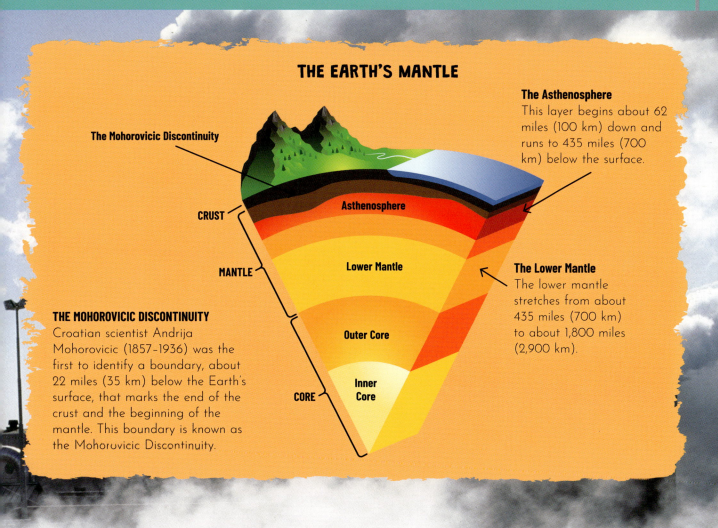

The Mohorovicic Discontinuity

The Asthenosphere
This layer begins about 62 miles (100 km) down and runs to 435 miles (700 km) below the surface.

CRUST

Asthenosphere

MANTLE

Lower Mantle

The Lower Mantle
The lower mantle stretches from about 435 miles (700 km) to about 1,800 miles (2,900 km).

Outer Core

THE MOHOROVICIC DISCONTINUITY
Croatian scientist Andrija Mohorovicic (1857-1936) was the first to identify a boundary, about 22 miles (35 km) below the Earth's surface, that marks the end of the crust and the beginning of the mantle. This boundary is known as the Mohoruvicic Discontinuity.

CORE

Inner Core

Lower Mantle

The lower mantle is made mostly of silicate rocks (rocks composed of silica, oxygen and metals). There is also a lot of iron and magnesium. Moving toward the core, both pressure and heat increase. At the edge of the core, temperatures may reach 2,200°C (3,992°F).

Old Faithful
At Yellowstone National Park in Wyoming, USA, the energy from a hot spot is believed to feed the park's many hot springs and pools. Old Faithful, one of the parks geysers, shoots about 31,800 litres (8,400 gallons) of boiling water into the air every 76 minutes.

The Earth's Core

Earth's core is the layer that scientists know the least about. They believe it is made up of two layers – an outer, molten liquid layer and a solid inner layer.

The Earth's outer core is made mainly of molten iron and nickel. It is 1367 miles (2,200 km) thick.

Earth's inner core is thought to be made of metals such as iron and nickel, too. Because the materials are under great pressure at this depth, the core stays solid.

At the inner core temperatures may be as high as 5,000°C (9,032°F). That is just slightly less than the temperature on the surface of the Sun.

This is a meteorite from Canyon Diablo in Arizona, USA. The meteorite is made of iron and nickel – the same ingredients as the Earth's core.

A blacksmith heats metal to make a horseshoe. The red-hot metal looks like lava and becomes soft. It behaves just like the metals of the Earth's outer core.

Earth's Core and its Magnetic Field

Earth's outer core is molten metal. As this mass moves, it spins the solid inner core of the planet. Scientists believe this motion, along with the core's heat, creates an electric current. That current creates a magnetic field around the planet. Earth behaves like a giant magnet.

The magnetic field that surrounds Earth is called the magnetosphere. It is a powerful force. It is the force that makes a compass point north.

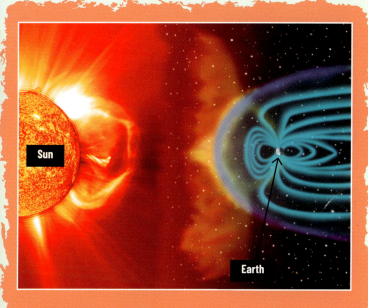

Sun

Earth

Our Protective Shield

The magnetosphere has several important jobs. Among them is to act as a protective layer for the planet. It keeps out harmful materials from space, including solar wind. Solar wind is a flow of particles from the Sun. Like magnets, these particles have a charge. If these particles reached Earth, they could be destructive. Thanks to the magnetosphere, that does not happen often. This artwork shows the magnetosphere (blue) forcing the particles (orange) out and around the planet.

MAKE A TREASURE MAP

Follow these simple steps to use a compass to create a treasure map for your friends to follow.

1) Stand with the compass in your hand. You should hold it as level as you can. Turn the bezel (the outside ring of the compass) so that north or zero lines up with the north-pointing arrow.

2) Pick a point a short distance away. Turn your body towards that point, looking at it over the compass bezel. The direction indicated on the bezel (for example, east) is the direction that you will be walking in to get to that point.

3) Mark the place you are starting from then walk the distance to your destination, noting the number of steps you take. Record the direction and the number of steps from your starting point (for example, 40 steps east). Now repeat steps 2 and 3 until you have created a route (for example 40 steps east,. 10 steps north, 5 steps west. 12 steps south.)

4) Place something to mark the spot of your final destination – your treasure spot. Record all of your directions, along with the number of steps to be taken from one point to the next, on a map.

5) Ask a friend to follow your 'treasure map', using the compass.

!

The compass is an old tool. Compasses were used by sailors and travellers to check the direction they were travelling in.

3. OUR RESTLESS EARTH

Look at a map of the world. Do you think it's possible that if there was no ocean between the continents the landmasses might fit together? For example, would the west of Africa fit around the north of South America?

Pangaea

In the late 1800s, and early 1900s, scientists began to study this idea. They investigated the idea that the Earth's continents were once a single huge piece of land. In 1912, German scientist Alfred Wegener (1880-1930) named this giant landmass 'Pangaea'.

EARTH'S JIGSAW

PANGAEA

The idea of continental drift suggests that about 250 million years ago, all of Earth's landforms were one continent. Scientists called this continent Pangaea. The name means 'all lands.'

GONDWANALAND AND LAURASIA

By about 200 million years ago, Pangaea had split into two smaller masses. Gondwanaland included land that would become the southern hemisphere. Laurasia included land that would become most of the northern hemisphere.

Continental Drift

In time, Pangaea split apart, and separate landmasses formed. These landmasses eventually became the continents we know today. This theory is now known as continental drift. Over millions of years the continents have drifted to their current positions. And they are still moving!

Scientists have gathered evidence to support this theory. They have discovered similar fossils on landmasses now separated by oceans. They have evidence of glaciers in places where today's climate does not suggest the presence of ice. They are able to show that the continents appear to 'fit together'.

CONTINENTAL DRIFT: FOSSIL EVIDENCE

The theory of continental drift answered the question of how similar fossils ended up on separate continents. Fossils of a prehistoric reptile called Mesosaurus had been found in the southern ends of both South America and Africa. The idea that the continents were once joined would explain how this freshwater reptile could be found in these two distant locations.

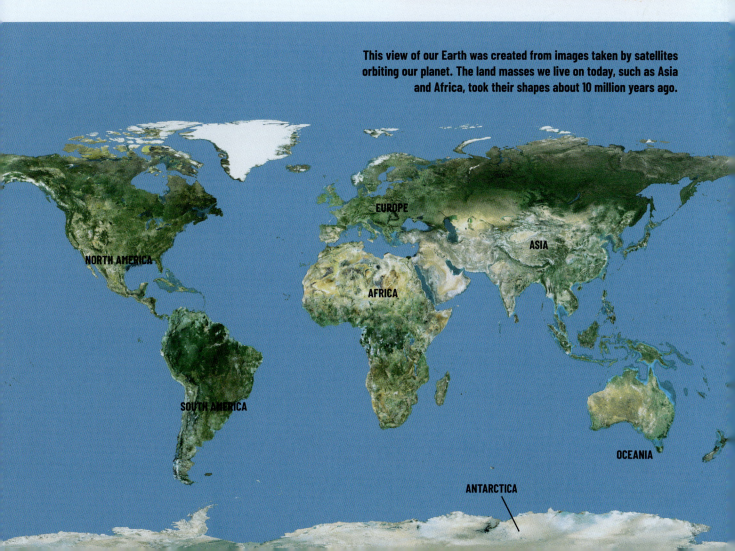

This view of our Earth was created from images taken by satellites orbiting our planet. The land masses we live on today, such as Asia and Africa, took their shapes about 10 million years ago.

EUROPE

ASIA

NORTH AMERICA

AFRICA

SOUTH AMERICA

OCEANIA

ANTARCTICA

EARTH'S TECTONIC PLATES

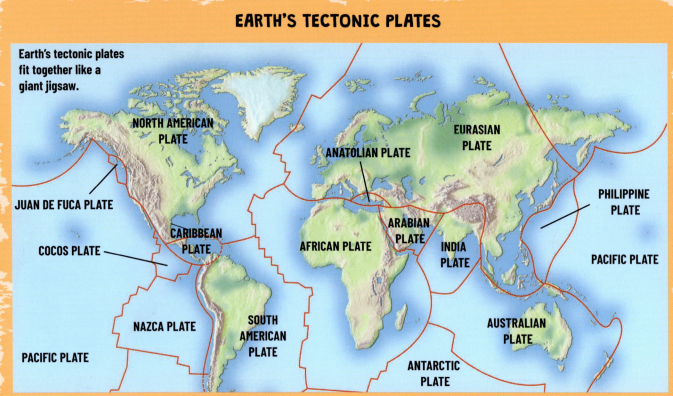

Earth's tectonic plates fit together like a giant jigsaw.

NORTH AMERICAN PLATE

JUAN DE FUCA PLATE

COCOS PLATE

CARIBBEAN PLATE

NAZCA PLATE

PACIFIC PLATE

SOUTH AMERICAN PLATE

ANTARCTIC PLATE

ANATOLIAN PLATE

EURASIAN PLATE

AFRICAN PLATE

ARABIAN PLATE

INDIA PLATE

AUSTRALIAN PLATE

PHILIPPINE PLATE

PACIFIC PLATE

Today, the continents are still moving. North America and Europe are slowly drifting apart at a rate of about 1.5 cm (0.6 inches) each year. The Atlantic and Indian Oceans get wider by 2.5 cms or so each year, while the Pacific Ocean is very slowly shrinking.

Cities on the Move

SAN ANDREAS FAULT

SAN FRANCISCO

LOS ANGELES

MOVEMENT OF THE NORTH AMERICAN PLATE

MOVEMENT OF THE PACIFIC PLATE

On the west coast of the USA, two tectonic plates meet along the San Andreas Fault. The two plates are moving past each other at an average rate of about 5cms (2 inches) each year.

In around 11 million years the cities of San Francisco and Los Angeles could be next to each other!

Plate Tectonics

The Earth's crust and the rigid upper section of the mantle are known together as the lithosphere, which is broken into huge, rigid pieces, called tectonic plates.

The tectonic plates support the continents and oceans, but they are constantly moving. They float on the oozing, liquid mantle below – moving just a few inches each year.

Scientists now know that much of the change in Earth's crust is caused by the movement of the plates in the lithosphere.

Faults

As tectonic plates slowly move, they squeeze and stretch the rocks underground. This creates an enormous amount of pressure to build up, which sometimes causes cracks to appear in Earth's crust. The places where the crust cracks are called faults.

The San Andreas fault is a 746 miles (1,200 km) long fault that runs along the Pacific coast of the USA.

EARTH'S CRACKED-UP CRUST

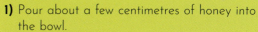

Materials needed

- Clear glass mixing bowl
- Clear honey
- Crackers

1) Pour about a few centimetres of honey into the bowl.
2) Carefully drop the crackers onto the honey.

3) Imagine that the honey is the Earth's liquid mantle and the crackers are the tectonic plates. What do you observe happening?

! Earth's temperature gets hotter toward the centre. The material also gets denser (thicker). This is what makes it possible for the mantle to support the crust even in its slightly melted state.

4) Now push one cracker with your finger. How easily does it move across the surface of the honey? What do you observe when one cracker moves against another?

! Moving one piece of cracker in the honey moves others – sometimes whether they touch or not. Earth's plates also affect one another as they move.

Earth's Ring of Fire

Earth has over 500 active volcanoes. An 'active' volcano is one that has erupted in recorded history. This total does not include the volcanoes in the oceans. Counting them would increase the total by a lot. Many volcanoes are located along a path called the 'Ring of Fire.' This very active line of volcanoes is around the boundaries of the Pacific Plate. There is also a lot of earthquake activity here.

The 'Ring of Fire' is shown in orange.

4. THE CHANGING FACE OF EARTH

Very active forces came together to create the Earth. Many of those forces continue to affect the planet today. Volcanic eruptions and earthquakes are natural events that affect and shape the planet's surface. They are also signs of activity within the planet's crust, mantle, and core.

Volcanoes

Earth is dotted with volcanoes. Some are on land and some lie under the oceans. Many of Earth's volcanoes occur along the edges of tectonic plates.

Some volcanoes erupt along the ocean ridges as plates move apart. Others form where an ocean plate meets a continental plate. Some simply rise up in the middle of a plate. These are created by hot spots.

INSIDE A VOLCANO

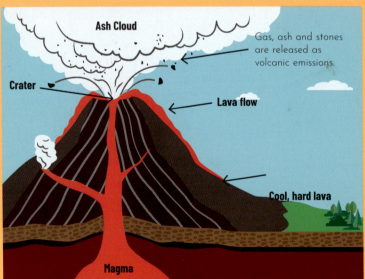

A volcano is a self-made mountain. Its hollow centre provides a pathway between the mantle and the surface. The sides of the volcano grow steeper as the lava from each eruption builds up.

Volcanoes are of special interest to scientists. A volcano's lava provides a direct look at material from inside our planet. It also gives evidence of processes taking place miles below the Earth's crust.

Islands in the Making

Volcanoes that occur under the oceans sometimes form islands. Every time a volcano erupts it grows bigger, until one day it breaks the water's surface, forming a volcanic island. The Hawaiian Islands were formed this way.

IDENTIFYING LAVA

Lava takes different forms. It can be smooth, or crumbly, or even formed from big blocky chunks. The form lava takes depends on:

- What it is made of
- How much gas is in it
- The temperature of the flow

Pahoehoe Flow
Lava that looks smooth and rope-like.

Aa Flow
Lava that is coarse and maybe sticky!

Pillow Flow
Lava that flows underwater.

FAULT LINES

During an earthquake, the Earth's crust can break along a fault. The rock on either side of the fault shifts, either sideways or up/down.

Normal Fault

A normal fault occurs when plates diverge, or move away from each other.

Reverse Fault (dip-slip)

A reverse fault occurs when plates converge or move toward one another.

Slip Fault (strike-slip)

A slip fault occurs when plates move past one another in a horizontal, or side-by-side, path.

Earthquakes

An earthquake begins with a build up of stress along a fault. The two sides of a fault are trying to slip past each other but they get stuck. Stress builds underground and the crust bends and flexes. Sometimes the bending and flexing does not relieve the tension. Suddenly, far underground, rocks break and give way. Vibrations called seismic waves are sent out. They make the ground on the surface shake violently, causing an earthquake.

Seismograms

Seismographs respond to ground noises and movement, such as shaking in an earthquake. Formerly data was recorded on paper or film but is now recorded digitally.

Tsunamis

Earthquakes can occur at faults underwater too. When they do, this can cause a tsunami – a giant wave. The water absorbs the energy of the earthquake and waves ripple out from the earthquake's epicentre – the place on the Earth's surface directly above where the earthquake starts.

The waves can move out across the ocean as fast as 497 miles per hour (800 km/h). At this point, the waves may be small, but as they approach land and move into shallower waters, they slow and start to build. Tsunami waves that hit a shore can be up to 30 meters (100 feet) tall!

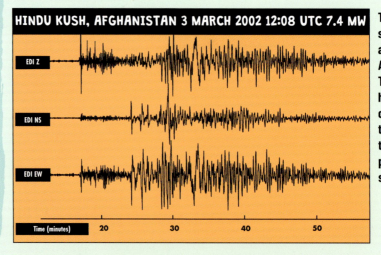

HINDU KUSH, AFGHANISTAN 3 MARCH 2002 12:08 UTC 7.4 MW

EDI Z

EDI NS

EDI EW

Time (minutes)   20   30   40   50

This is the seismogram of an earthquake in Afghanistan in 2002. The earthquake had a magnitude of 7.4. The bigger the earthquake, the bigger the peaks traced on the seismogram.

Rescue workers and survivors search in the rubble of a city following an earthquake in August 2007. The earthquake in Pisco, Peru had a magnitude of 8.

Measuring Earthquakes

The strength, or magnitude, of an earthquake is measured by scientists using a scale called the Moment Magnitude Scale. An earthquake of magnitude 'one' can only be detected by sensitive equipment. An earthquake with a magnitude of 8 is considered devastating! One of the world's largest earthquake was recorded in Chile on 22nd May, 1960. It had a magnitude of 9.5. Thousands of people were killed or injured, and two million people lost their homes.

MAGMA UNDER PRESSURE

Materials needed:

• A tube of toothpaste   • A wooden skewer

Using a tube of toothpaste, explore how magma moves around inside the Earth's crust, mantle, and core.

1) Make sure the top to the toothpaste tube is screwed on tight.

2) Use your thumbs and fingers to put pressure on the tube in different places. Observe how the contents of the tube move away from the pressure.

3) Now use the skewer to poke a small hole in the toothpaste tube. Squeeze again. The hole provides the trapped 'magma' with a way to release the pressure.

Magma is often under pressure in the Earth from factors such as heat and layers of weight from above. When that happens, the molten rock will seek the nearest open space. The magma escapes and relieves the pressure.

MAKING MOUNTAINS

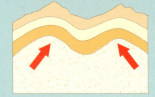

Fold Mountains

Sometimes the plate movements can force rocks to push against each other, fold and rise up. Mountains are pushed up at upfolds and valleys form in downfolds.

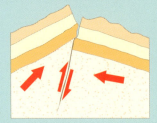

Fault Mountains

Sometimes the Earth's surface cracks on a fault. Layers of rock on one side of the fault can be pushed up to form a mountain.

Volcanic Mountains

Some mountains are formed by volcanic activity. Volcanic mountains are formed from lava and rocks. After a volcanic eruption, the lava hardens and cools on the surface.

Dome Mountains

Sometimes heat from inside the mantle pushes the Earth's crust upward. This creates a bulge on the surface.

An Ever-changing Picture

The Earth's crust is constantly changing. Natural forces, such as heat, pressure, and movement from within the Earth cause these changes. On the surface, weather and erosion cause changes. But it is a long, slow process.

Mountains

Mountains are one of Earth's constantly changing features. Mountains are formed when the Earth's tectonic plates move. As the plates collide or move against each other, their boundaries deform. This causes huge, rocky landforms to appear on the Earth's surface - mountains. It can take thousands or millions of years for a mountain to form.

Weathering and Erosion

The Earth's crust is also shaped by outside forces such as weathering and erosion. Weathering is the gradual break down of rock. Over time, wind, water and other surface factors wear away the rock's surface until it crumbles. Then erosion takes over. Wind, water and even ice carry or blow the sediment away. This rock formation is the Three Gossips in Arches Park, Utah, USA. It shows the results of weathering and erosion over time.

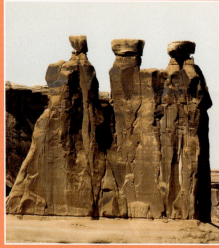

The Andes are the world's longest chain of mountains. They were formed around 70 million years ago when the Nazca plate collided with the South American plate.

Water at Work

Water is another factor in the constant change of Earth's surface. Rivers make huge changes to the landscape. As a river runs its course it can carve a deep valley into the Earth's crust. It can also carry sediment from one place and deposit it in another. The ocean changes the edges of the Earth's landmasses. It crashes into the shore and creates craggy cliffs.

The Gorges du Verdon is in France. This deep valley is being formed as the flowing Verdon River cuts its path. Notice the valley's V shape. A V-shaped valley is a sign of a young stream.

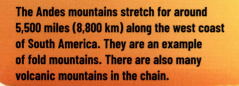

The Andes mountains stretch for around 5,500 miles (8,800 km) along the west coast of South America. They are an example of fold mountains. There are also many volcanic mountains in the chain.

MAKING TRENCHES

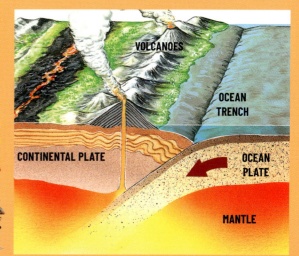

VOLCANOES

OCEAN TRENCH

CONTINENTAL PLATE

OCEAN PLATE

MANTLE

Sometimes the Earth's plates move toward one another, forcing one under the other. This is called subduction. In the ocean, this can result in deep trenches.

Marble is a metamorphic rock. It is formed when limestone comes under great heat and pressure. Its colours and grain have made it a popular material. In ancient times it was used for carving statues. Today, your kitchen surfaces might be marble.

5. EARTH'S BUILDING MATERIALS

The crust of our planet is made of rock. The tectonic plates move that rock. They crunch and fold it. They force rock from deep underground to the surface. Volcanoes heat up underground rocks and spew them out onto the surface. Rocks are constantly on the move and changing.

Types of Rock

The rocks of Earth's crust are made mainly from eight elements, but the way these elements combine creates many, many different kinds of rock. Scientists separate Earth's rocks into three groups.

Igneous rocks are formed from molten magma that has cooled and become solid.

These layered sandstone formations in Antelope Canyon, Arizona, USA, have been formed by erosion from powerful, rushing flood waters.

Soil: The Basis for Life

Because soil is everywhere, we sometimes forget how important it is. Without soil, plants couldn't grow.

Soil is created by weathering. Fine grains of rock and minerals combine with air, water, and organic materials. Soil varies throughout the world. But its basic ingredients remain the same.

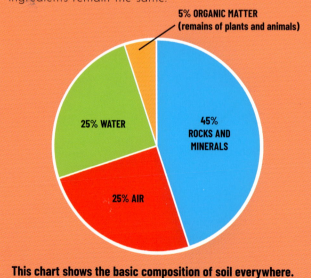

5% ORGANIC MATTER (remains of plants and animals)

25% WATER

45% ROCKS AND MINERALS

25% AIR

This chart shows the basic composition of soil everywhere.

THE ROCK CYCLE

The rock cycle is a constant process of change.
The rock cycle changes rocks from one type into another.
It is happening around us and under our feet all the time!

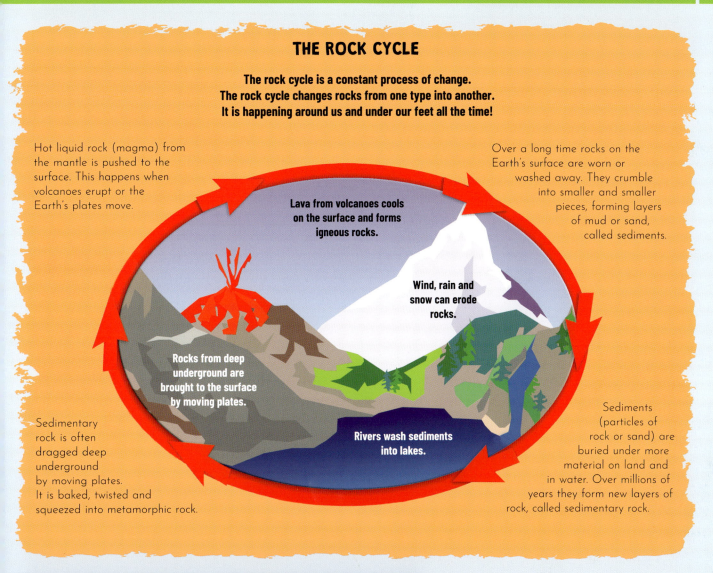

Hot liquid rock (magma) from the mantle is pushed to the surface. This happens when volcanoes erupt or the Earth's plates move.

Over a long time rocks on the Earth's surface are worn or washed away. They crumble into smaller and smaller pieces, forming layers of mud or sand, called sediments.

Lava from volcanoes cools on the surface and forms igneous rocks.

Wind, rain and snow can erode rocks.

Rocks from deep underground are brought to the surface by moving plates.

Sedimentary rock is often dragged deep underground by moving plates. It is baked, twisted and squeezed into metamorphic rock.

Rivers wash sediments into lakes.

Sediments (particles of rock or sand) are buried under more material on land and in water. Over millions of years they form new layers of rock, called sedimentary rock.

This granite mountain shows signs of another changing process called exfoliation. This is the process by which whole sheets of rock break off. The rock is then broken up into sediments. The waterfalls and streams in the mountains carry the sediment away.

Metamorphic rocks form deep underground. Heat, pressure, and magma change these rocks. The structure and makeup of the original rock may be completely changed.

Sedimentary rocks are formed from layers of sediment (tiny grains of rock). These rocks can form on land or in water. They form wherever sediment is deposited. Over many years, the sediments are crushed until they join together and form rocks.

SCIENTISTS IN ACTION

Figuring out Earth's mysteries takes many brains and many ideas. Some of the scientists involved in these studies include:

Geologists

Geologists study Earth's structure, including the study of rocks and their formations.

Hydrogeologists

Hydrogeologists study how water (hydro) moves through the Earth's soil and rocks (geology).

Mineralogists

These professional 'rock collectors' study rocks, gemstones and other minerals.

Seismologists

Seismologists study earthquakes and seismic waves.

Volcanologists

Volcanologists study old volcanic deposits, new eruptions, the insides of volcanoes, magma and lava. With modern equipment volcanologists can predict future eruptions. This can help to save thousands of lives!

Still Searching for Answers

Technology in science is quickly improving our study of Earth's crust and core. Every day, it seems, we improve our ability to investigate our world. After an earthquake, for example, the Internet now offers information on the event for scientists worldwide. The location of the earthquake's epicentre, its magnitude, and its length and depth along a fault line are readily available.

Scientific Forecasting

It used to be that we wanted to find out if a volcano was going to erupt or if an earthquake might occur. Scientists now want to be able to tell when. They want to be able to forecast.

When a volcano erupts, scientists want to know who or what might be in its path. How much warning do people need to get out of the way? With the help of computer software, scientists are able to look at a volcano's pattern of eruptions, its shape, changes in that shape, and other details. This information is then used to forecast the next eruption – often accurately.

Learning anything about Earth is a matter of building upon ideas - yours, a fellow scientist's, history's. Who knows where the next 'big idea' will come from?

Seeing Earth as a System

Very few events take place on Earth without affecting life around them. An earthquake causes a tsunami that crushes a coastline. A plate collides with another and folds into a mountain...
Scientists have begun to look at Earth as a single system. They see everything as connected.

NASA in the USA has a programme to look at this. It is called Earth Science Programme. It overlaps different sciences to study the land, water, and air.

The programme has three parts:

1) Satellites to watch the planet and collect information.

2) A system to review the information.

3) A team of scientists to study the information.

A team of geologists reach the summit crater of Mount Erebus in December 2005. Mount Erebus is the most active volcano in Antarctica. It has a molten lake of lava at the bottom of the crater. Steam can be seen rising from the crater.

SG 3

The former USSR is among the countries that have attempted deep drilling projects. The Soviets' goal was to investigate the Earth's crust through deep drilling. They began drilling on 24th May, 1970, at the Kola Peninsula in the Arctic. They drilled for 24 years and dug a hole 7.5 miles (12 km) deep. The Russians did not get through the crust as they had hoped. But they did get rocks from a deeper part of the crust than anyone before had. Geologists had theories of what rocks at this depth would be like. They were able to compare actual rocks with their theories. The hole, named SG-3, is still the deepest hole ever made by humans.

Kola Peninsula

URAL MOUNTAINS

UK

EUROPE

ALPS

BLACK SEA

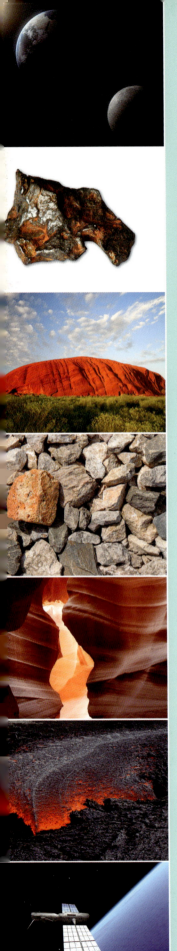

GLOSSARY

asthenosphere The thin, pliable layer of Earth's upper mantle on which the rigid crust can move.

atmosphere The thick layer of air that surrounds the Earth. The gases that make up Earth's atmosphere include nitrogen (78%) and oxygen (21%). There is also water, and small quantities of other gases such as argon, greenhouse gases and carbon dioxide.

atom All materials and subtances are made up of atoms. They are the smallest possible unit of an element that still behaves like that element.

core The core is the centre layer of the Earth's three layers. It is made up on an inner and an outer core. The Earth's core is about 2,100 miles (3,400 km) thick.

crust The outer layer of the Earth. The crust is about 25 miles (40 km) thick beneath the continental landmasses and 4 miles (7 km) thick beneath the oceans.

diameter The distance measured by a straight line through the centre of a circle or sphere.

earthquake A violent shaking of the ground. It is caused by rocks deep underground cracking and breaking when they are put under stress due to movements of the Earth's tectonic plates.

elements Substances made up of a single type of atom. Elements can't be broken into simpler components by chemical processes. There are 92 naturally occurring elements, such as Hydrogen (H), Iron (Fe) and Silicon (Si). Some elements are liquid, some are gases, and some are solids.

erosion To carry away material by movement of wind, water or ice.

faults Cracks in the Earth's crust. The movement of the Earth's tectonic plates causes rocks to move and stretch until the pressure becomes so great that they crack.

fossils The remains of a once living thing, such as an animal or plant, preserved in rock.

glacier A huge, slow-moving river of ice, usually around 30 metres (100 feet) thick. The glacier moves slowly down a slope or valley. Some glaciers move only a 2.5cm to 5 cms a year. Others travel up to 1 metre (3 feet) a day.

global warming A gradual warming of the Earth's atmosphere. Most scientists believe that this is caused by humans burning fossils fuels, such as oil and coal. The burning of these fuels gives off greenhouse gases that are trapping too much of the Sun's heat in the Earth's atmosphere.

Gondwanaland One of two landmasses thought to have formed when Pangaea broke apart some 200 million years ago. It is made up of land that now forms the continents of Africa, Antarctica, Australia, Asia, and South America.

greenhouse gases Gases such as carbon dioxide, methane and nitrous oxide. These gases trap heat from the Sun in the Earth's atmosphere – a lot like the glass roof of a greenhouse traps the Sun's heat.

igneous rock Rocks formed from magma that has reached the Earth's surface and cooled. To remember that igneous rocks are caused by great heat and fire, think of the word 'ignite'.

landform A feature on Earth's surface such as a mountain.

Laurasia One of two landmasses formed by the breakup of Pangaea some 200 million years ago. Laurasia was made up of land that now forms Europe, North America, and parts of Asia.

lava Molten material made of rock, gas and other debris that comes from an erupting volcano. Before it reaches the surface, this material is known as magma.

lithosphere The hard outer layer of the Earth formed from the crust and the uppermost part of the mantle. On average, the lithosphere is about 60 miles (100 km) deep. The word lithosphere comes from the Greek word 'lithos', which means 'stone'.

magma The fiery, flowing mix of rock found in Earth's mantle and outer core. The heat and pressure inside the Earth keeps the material in this semifluid state. When magma manages to escape to the surface of the planet, it is called lava.

mantle The Earth's middle layer. The mantle has an average thickness of 1,800 miles (2,900 km).

metamorphic rock Rock that has been transformed into a different type of rock. Most metamorphic rock forms because of great heat and pressure deep within the Earth. To remember this process think of the word 'morph', which means 'to change'.

Moment Magnitude Scale A system used by scientists to measure the strength and size of an earthquake.

orbit When one object, such as a planet, makes a complete circuit around another object, such as the Sun, usually on a circular or oval path. This movement is continuous.

Pangaea The name given to the large land mass that existed about 250 million years ago. Pangaea was made up of all the land masses that form the individual continents we live on today. The existence of Pangaea is part of the theory of continental drift.

planet Any large body in space that revolves around a star as part of a solar system. Earth's solar system includes eight major planets: Mercury, Venus, Earth, Mars, Jupiter, Saturn, Uranus, Neptune.

plate tectonics The study of the movements of the Earth's tectonic plates.

satellite A body that revolves around another larger body in space. The Moon is Earth's only natural satellite.

sedimentary rock A rock formed from layers of sediment. Over many years, pressure from the layers above combined with heat packs the sediment together until they form new rock.

solar system A group of planets orbiting a star, such as our Sun.

tectonic plates The giant jigsaw-like pieces of the Earth's crust. The plates float on the Earth's mantle and are constantly moving at a very slow rate.

tsunami A Japanese word for the huge and damaging ocean waves caused by earthquake vibrations under the ocean.

volcano A hole in the Earth's crust through which gas, ash, and magma escape from the mantle. Volcanic eruptions cause a mountain to form made from lava that has cooled and hardened.

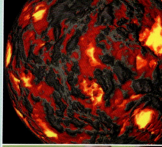

INDEX